The Real Terrorists:

Lock Them All Up

ATRANE

Table of Contents

Introduction

Chapter 1: Barack Obama

It was the end of December 2016 and Barack Obama decided to retaliate against Russia after the alleged reports of the "Russian hacking" that influenced the elections in the United States. He didn't even bother to wait for the official investigative report on the allegations to hit his desk in the Oval Office. Instead, he rushed to impose new sanctions against Russian and expel 35 intelligence operatives from American soil.

Let's take a look back at the April 2015. It was then when Obama issued an executive order that indirectly excludes the option of taking counteroffensive measures against foreign cyber-actions aimed at the U.S. electoral system. Obama himself included the term that requires "harm to critical infrastructure or the theft or commercial secrets" for any action to be taken.

That means that Obama and his associates considered electoral infrastructure as critical and that the Russians actually did harm it. The officials did say that the hackers hired by the Russian government penetrated at least one state's database of registered voters. However, they confirmed that the hackers didn't tamper with any data. Despite that, Obama made legal adjustments needed to enforce the sanctions on Russia. Not only that, but the previous Administration did everything it could to make it harder for Donald Trump to reverse any of their actions once he arrives at the office.

Even if you think that Obama was protecting the country and you justify the sanctions against Russia, you have to ask yourself this: Why the Department of Homeland Security didn't face the same wrath as Russians?

Brian Kemp, Georgia Secretary of State, accused the DHS of attempting to breach the state's database of registered voters in November 2016. The investigation conducted by the State of Georgia linked the IP address of the attack back to the federal DHS. Kemp asked for an explanation on multiple occasions but failed to get one from the Secretary of DHS Jeh Johnson. Believe it or not, Johnson blamed it all on misconfiguration on one of the employee's computers. An official investigation was never conducted and Obama completely ignored the issue.

If Obama claims that each state's database of voters is a 'critical infrastructure', why didn't he investigate the issue in Georgia? Or is this a double standard and Obama just wanted to prosecute the Russians and deepen the gap in relations with that country?

Antonia Okafor is a passionate black graduate student and a two-time Obama voter. She said in an interview with the Daily Caller News Foundation in January 2017 that she is disappointed with how Obama handled race relations during his presidency. Okafor believed that he is the best choice for her simply because he looks like her. She was disappointed to see that Obama was just using false political narratives to win the elections. He didn't care about the African-American community, he only cared about how he could use them to get to the political power.

Although Barack Obama was the first American black president, race relations between white and black people got much worse during his presidency. Let's take a look at the timeline of race relations under Obama:

- In 2009, Harvard professor Henry Louis Gates arrived home and discovered his front door lock jammed. He decided to force his way through the back door, but worried neighbors weren't sure what's going on and in good faith alerted the police. When the officers arrived, they asked Gates for an ID. He became infuriated for no reason, shouting "That's what it means to be black in America! Do you know how many graduate degrees I have? Can you even spell Harvard?" The officers arrested him for disorderly conduct. When asked about the incident, Obama said that the white working-class officer "acted stupidly", completely disregarding the facts.

- In 2012, Hispanic-American George Zimmerman called the police when he noticed a young black man, Trayvon Martin, urinating in front of a house. Although Zimmerman said the police he suspected Martin to be on drugs (autopsy confirmed this), he got the instructions not to pursue the suspect. A little later, Martin attacked Zimmerman and started pounding his head into the pavement. Zimmerman somehow reached for the gun and killed Martin. Obama's only comment was "If I had a son, he would look like Trayvon". Would that mean he would be on drugs knocking people's heads into pavements?

Later on, Zimmerman was released, which led to riots across the country. The random white guy was robbed while the assailants yelled: "This is for Trayvon".

- In November 2013, police officers shot and killed Kimani Gray, a 16-year old black teenager from Brooklyn, New York. Although it was only after Gray drew a firearm directly at them, making the action completely justifiable, the incident caused new riots. Shops across Brooklyn were looted and windows smashed.

- In August 2014, 18-year old black teenager Michael Brown robbed a convenience store. A police officer named Darren Wilson pulled him over when Brown tried to grab his gun. The young man then retreated, but when Wilson tried to exit the vehicle, he sprinted towards him. He warned Brown a couple of times before shooting and killing him. The action as justifiable and he was acquitted by a grand jury.

Barack Obama claimed that "the shooting exposed racial divide that stains the heart of black children". CNN even reported that Brown had his hands up, shouting "don't shoot". That was a lie. Riots across Missouri lasted for weeks so the state had to pronounce a state of emergency.

- In 2015, the national spotlight turned to Baltimore. Freddie Gray died in the back of a police van as a result of spinal cord injuries, after being arrested for carrying an illegal switchblade. Obama added fuel to the fire of rumors that the death is a result of racism in policing. He claimed "This is not new. It has been going on for a long time, and we shouldn't pretend that it is new". Riots started in Baltimore, pharmacies were burned down and even firefighters were attacked on the job.

- In July 2016, Philandro Castile was killed by a Chinese police officer Jeronimo Yanez. The police officer was charged with second-degree manslaughter, but that didn't prevent the new riots. Obama said: ""When incidents like this occur, there's a big chunk of our citizenry that feels as if, because of the color of their skin, they are not being treated the same, and that hurts, and that should trouble all of us."

- In August 2016, 23-year old black male Sylville Smith was killed by a black police officer in Milwaukee. Racial agitators once again rioted, setting shops and police cars aflame. The justice system once again did its job when it charged the officer with homicide.

Okafor believes that Obama is not a peacemaker. Instead, he used every opportunity to amplify racial tensions. She claims that Obama had been calling for "race wars" to enable power and control to progressives. Okafor explains that it's much easier to wield control if you marginalize facts and logic. While fueling the racial tension through Obama, the elite kept the different point of views out of the media. That resulted in people protesting although the justice system worked and works perfectly.

The coalition led by the United States has been fighting ISIL by conducting airstrikes throughout Iraq and Syria since 2014. Until the end of 2016, the coalition had conducted more than 10,000 strikes in Iraq and over 6,000 in Syria. None of these strikes were backed by the UN Security Council or the official Syrian government. The official explanation is that the airstrikes are conducted to help alleged ground antiterror operations in Iraq and Syria. The truth is that the coalition led by the United States supports the opposition party in Syria and wants to see the official Syrian government gone.

Politics aside, the thing that makes everyone worried are the civilian casualties in the airstrikes. The US Combined Joint Task Force – Operation Inhered Resolve assessed that at least 188 civilians were unintentionally killed by coalition strikes since the start of the operation. Amnesty International fears that this number is far from accurate and that the total civilian death toll is over 300.

"CJTF-OIR regrets the unintentional loss of civilian lives resulting from coalition efforts to defeat ISIL in Iraq and Syria and express our deepest sympathies to the families and others affected by these strikes."

The coalition fails to mention what they will do to prevent further civilian casualties, claiming only that "sometimes casualties are unavoidable".

Former Pentagon official Michael Maloof explains:

"The United States is supposed to double-check and triple-check to make sure that not a single civilian is in danger. The reality suggests that we don't have intelligence and credible information from the ground. This is confirmed by the statements from the coalition, which claims that they have not-credible reports about the incidents involving casualties. That basically means that they don't have information to determine whether any civilians were killed or any actual collateral damage was made", says Maloof.

In practice, this means that the US-led coalition is bombing areas despite good intelligence from the ground. On December 29th, 2016, the task force targeted the van of the Islamic State militants. It was hit in what later turned out to be a hospital compound parking lot, resulting in possible civilian casualties.

Barack Obama didn't care about the loss of innocent lives. He approved attacks in Syria because global liberal elite wants the official Syrian government gone and that is the only goal they had in mind.

There were ten times more air strikes in the covert war on terror during President Barack Obama's presidency than under his predecessor, George W. Bush. Drone strikes are Obama's favored tactics of war. The problem is that many experts from around the world see this as state-sponsored targeted assassination.

"The United States has no right to conduct drone strikes. They are nothing but executions of suspected political adversaries. It contravenes international law", claims Rasmus Helveg Petersen from the Danish Social Liberal Party. The words carry even more weight if you know that Denmark has been side by side with the U.S. for decades.

Soren Pind, a member of Denmark's opposition Venstre party, also blasted Obama.

"I criticized Bush for something that could have been seen as torture, but Obama is combining the presidency with assassination. He is ignoring western world's principles", claims Pind.

Let's take a look at how a drone strike looks in practice. It was enough that Obama's administration declares the target a terrorist to justify an attack. It doesn't even matter if the targets are American citizens as we witnessed in 2016 when American-born Anwar al-Awlaki and his son were killed in a drone strike. Obama's lawyers confirmed in December 2016 that even U.S. citizens are legitimate military targets and do not have the right to any legal protection if they are at war with America.

Former Secretary of Defense Leon Panetta discovered during a CBS 60 minutes' interview that Obama personally approves the policy to kill American citizens suspected of terrorism, even though they weren't prosecuted!

UN special reporter on extrajudicial, summary or arbitrary executions Christof Heyns describes drone strikes as a violation of the international legal system and assesses that some attacks may constitute war crimes. Zamir Akram, Pakistan's UN ambassador in Geneva, noted that more than 1,000 civilians were killed in the US drone strikes in Pakistan.

"We find the use of drones to be totally counterproductive in terms of succeeding in the 'war on terror'. It leads to greater levels of terror rather than reducing them", says Akram.

The International Herald Tribune reports that experts all agree that the drone strikes are only serving to fuel hatred towards the United States. Too many innocent people getting killed is nothing more than a justification for future terrorist activities. That should be proof enough that Obama and the elite behind him don't want the war on terror to end, but they are actually trying to keep it going with all the attacks.

In a report from July 1st, 2016, Barack Obama claimed that U.S. drone strikes had killed no more than 64 "non-combatants" in Pakistan, Libya, Yemen and Somalia between January 2009 and the end of 2015. The Bureau of Investigative Journalism, on the other hand, notes anywhere between 380 to 801 civilian casualties. The Bureau's data is based on reports by local and international journalists, leaked government documents, NVO investigators, court papers and field investigations.

What strikes as weird is that the assessments of the minimum total number of people killed are remarkably similar. Obama's administration puts the figure at 2,436 while the Bureau notes 2,753 deaths. The count is incomplete because the reports didn't take into account drone strikes from Afghanistan, Iraq, and Syria. That means that, in reality, the death toll can be much bigger.

Shortly after Obama took the presidency he had to preside over a drone strike for the first time. On January 22, 2009, the strike missed its target and 10 civilians were killed, including one child. That didn't stop Obama from continuing the drone strikes and their number increased to 100 until the end of 2009. An even bigger incident occurred just prior to Obama getting into the White House. A CIA drone strike was launched on a funeral in Pakistan killing over 40 civilians. That also wasn't enough for Obama to rethink the wisdom of the U.S. approach.

During his presidency, Obama significantly extended the use of drones in the War on Terror. He embraced the US drone program and America conducted ten times more strikes during his two terms than under bush. Obama saw the use of drones as an option to keep up the war against Al Qaeda while avoiding ground wars in the Middle East and Asia. The White House insisted that drone strikes are "exceptionally surgical and precise and they don't put innocent men, women or children in danger". After some while and a lot of civilian casualties, the criticism of lethal drone strikes couldn't be neglected.

"The truth is that this technology really began to take off right at the beginning of my presidency. And it wasn't until about a year, year and a half in where I began to realize that the Pentagon and our national security apparatus and the CIA were all getting too comfortable with the technology as a tool to fight terrorism, and not being mindful enough about how that technology is being used. And so, we initiated this big process to try to get it in a box, and checks and balances, and much higher standards about when they're used ", said Obama in an interview for The Atlantic in January 2017.

The way of balancing Obama applied might explain the difference in the number of civilian casualties. Here is the method how Obama's administration decided who are civilians:

"All military-age males that are located in a strike zone are counted as combatants unless there is explicit intelligence posthumously proving their innocence."

That explains the absurdly low figures cited by Obama's officials. Another interesting thing to note is that Obama not only approved "personality" strikes aimed at high-value terrorist but also "signature" strikes that aimed at training camps and suspicious compounds. Certain State Department officials complained to the White House that the criteria CIA used were too lax. For example, men loading a truck with fertilizer could be bombmakers, but they could also be farmers. But these officials claim that for CIA they were always bombmakers.

Barack Obama tried to use the Christmas period in 2016 to quietly pass the "Intelligence Authorization Act for Fiscal Year 2017" bill into law. It doesn't come as strange that the bill was passed during Christmas as the people behind the legislation wanted to avoid public notice. The trouble with the bill is that it effectively labels alternative media as foreign propaganda and criminalizes it. Global Research Centre claims that this bill established the U.S. very own Ministry of Truth and puts all the media under federal control. There are two things you need to know about this bill:

- It claims that it will "criminalize fake news and propaganda on the Web". In practice, that means that the legislation restrains free speech and independent media. It allows the government to crack down with impunity against any media outlet it deems "propaganda". An independent journalist (or even a person that blogs out of fun) could easily face criminal charges if he is labeled as someone who is spreading foreign propaganda on his/her website.
- A substantial amount of money is provided to fund "counter propaganda". That means that huge sums of money will be invested to fund stories deemed as appropriate by the "Ministry of Truth"

The creators of the legislation are U.S. Senators Rob Portman and Chris Murphy. According to them, the bill has the goal of "protecting the freedom of the marketplace of ideas on the international stage", rather than dealing with alternative news sources within America. The legislation includes the part where an inter-agency body will "track and evaluate counterfactual narratives abroad that threaten the national security interests of the United States and United States allies". It will also develop "procedures to expose and refute foreign misinformation and disinformation and proactively promote fact-based narratives and policies to audiences outside the United States."

While this might be good news for domestic journalists, it still means that the goal of this bill was for the Obama's government to manipulate the media coverage and shape public opinion throughout the world. And who's to say that it won't also be used for domestic purposes?

In September 2016, a leaked audio in which Secretary of State John Kerry can be heard talking to the leaders of Syrian opposition groups appeared. There were some very interesting revelations that should open our eyes when it comes to Obama's government. The most important thing of all is that the only goal that the United States had in Syria was to overthrow Bashar el-Assad, the current president of the country. Kerry's conversation with two dozen Syrians featured in the leaked audio took place during the U.N. General Assembly in 2016. You can find the audio online (check out the references section for a link or simply use Google search).

In order to accomplish the regime change, Obama and his staff were willing to watch the Islamic State grow. They were placing their bet on ISIS, hoping that their success wild force Assad to step down.

The White House even went one step further and delivered a lot of weapons to ISIS. That Obama's government responsible for the loss of thousands of lives during the civil war in Syria, which has already been lasting for several years and nobody knows when it will end.

Another proof of Obama's use of so-called "war on terror" to achieve the liberal elite goals and objectives is that the White House admitted to carrying out an air strike that killed more than 60 Syrian soldiers. The American government did that to stop the military convoy and stop a strategic attack upon the Islamic extremists. Kerry admits in the leaked audio that the only thing they didn't calculate is that Assad would turn to Russia for help.

"We knew ISIS was growing, we were watching, we saw that DAESH (ISIS) was growing in strength, and we thought Assad was threatened. We thought that we could manage to get Assad into negotiations, but instead of that, he got Putin to support him".

Obama gave a press conference in 2014 where he stated that the White House "did not have a strategy against ISIS". In fact, they did and it involved delivering arms to them and letting them do the dirty work of the regime change, not caring how many people will die in the process.

Hillary Clinton also aided the rise of ISIS, which is explained later in the book.

Judicial Watch published documents that connect the U.S. Ambassador Christopher Stevens to shipping weapons from Benghazi to support al-Qaida-affiliated militias fighting the regime of Bashar el-Assad in Syria. That way the United States were directly arming the Sunni jihadists who later turned into ISIS.

Stevens was killed in a terrorist attack in Benghazi in 2012, which aimed to kill "as many American citizens as possible". Al-Qaida performed the attack with the goal of forcing the U.S. to release Omar Abdul Rahman, the "blind sheik" serving a life sentence in a prison in America. A much bigger scandal is the fact that all American top officials, including Hillary Clinton and Barack Obama, knew about the attack. In fact, World Net Daily (WND) revealed in an article that James "Ace" Lyons, a former four-star admiral and founding member of the Citizens' Commission on Benghazi, provided evidence that Obama's administration orchestrated the attack!

Lyons claims that the White House wanted to find a way to release the "blind sheik" that will make the decision justifiable in the eyes of the public. They wanted to release the sheik to comply with a request Egyptian President Mohamed Morsi made during his acceptance speech in 2012. Obama's administration decided to offer the al-Qaida-affiliated rebels who were working with the Libyan Muslim Brotherhood an opportunity to kidnap Stevens and then exchange him for the sheik. Unfortunately, the plan went wrong and Stevens was killed.

CIA claimed that the attack on the compound was not well organized. However, Michael Morell, former CIA deputy director, offers his view on the "real-time" video of the attack.

"That would mean that the extremists managed to gather a group of like-minded individuals with little or no planning. You can see signs of a well-thought-out plan and organization, as well as command and control. There were no heavy weapons on the videotape. Many of the attackers, after entering the front gate, ran past buildings to the other end of the compound. They didn't seem like they are looking Americans to harm, they appeared to be intent on looting and conducting vandalism", explains Morell in his book "The Great War of Our Time".

Despite the fact that Morell claimed CIA was lying, Obama's administration didn't release the 'real-time' video of the attack, adding further doubt to what happened in the compound and why was the U.S. Ambassador killed.

Chapter 2: Hillary Clinton

She Gave the Direct Order to Kill Waco Babies

Hillary Clinton was considered an appropriate candidate for the U.S. elections by the global elite. This wasn't the first time she was the 'right person' for doing the job of executing the intentions of the elite. She was also instructed to oversee the destruction of Libya, where more than 100,000 lives were lost for no good reason. Clinton also did a lot of damage in her own country. She is personally to blame for deaths of more than 80 men, women, and children in Waco, Texas, in 1993!

On February 28th, 1993, federal agents attempted to arrest David Koresh, the leader of the Branch Davidians, who was accused of stockpiling weapons. The raid of the religious set's compound in Waco was unsuccessful and ended with a gun battle in which six cult members and four agents lost their lives. However, this is just a beginning of a sad story.

A two-month long siege of the compound was to follow after the unsuccessful raid. Although not ideal, the situation was peaceful when Hillary Clinton decided to stir things up. Former White House aide Linda Tripp said in an interview that Clinton pressured the White House counsel Vincent Foster to resolve the standoff. It was her direct order that Foster was executing when he instructed another raid on the Branch Davidians' compound on April 19, 1993.

The federal agents attacked the compound that night using tear gas. A fire soon broke out and the wooden barracks started to burn. Koresh and about 20 other cult members shot themselves to death as the fire was spreading through the compound. 60 more people died in the fire or in the collapsed buildings, bringing the total death toll to 80 Branch Davidians. Only 11 members of the religious sect managed to safely escape from the compound.

Even though she gave him a direct order, Clinton marked Foster as the main person to blame for the massacre. She started mercilessly ridiculing him in front of its peers claiming that he failed 'them'. Former FBI agent Jim Clemente claims that there were detailed reports about these incidents. However, when he decided to look for them in the National Archives, it was determined that the reports had gone missing. Vince Foster killed himself later in 1993.

Mike McNulty, the author of the Academy Award nominated documentary Waco: Rules of Engagement and two more movies about the massacre, also believes that Hillary Clinton is the one who gave a direct order. Her role in the assault on the campus has never been fully disclosed. A cover-up and Foster's suicide that followed make things even more suspicious. The late McNulty confirmed to have information indicating that Clinton was involved and in command, directing the FBI's actions from the White House, and leading the cover-up after the massacre.

The best way to explain Trans-Pacific Partnership (TTP) is to use NAFTA, the North American Free Trade Agreement signed by the United States, Mexico, and Canada. The treaty was signed by Bill Clinton. NAFTA is already the biggest free trade agreement in the world, and TTP would represent a bigger version of it. TTP is planned to cover 12 Asian-Pacific countries, including the three that are also part of NAFTA. The TTP treaty has been a subject of numerous debates during the last decade and Hillary Clinton was part of those discussions several times.

"Greater economic integration will bring us big benefits. We know that that can help us create new jobs and opportunities here at home", said Clinton in 2010 when she was a secretary of state.

"TTP is a cutting-edge, next generation trade deal that eliminates all trade tariffs and improves supply change, saves energy and enhances business practices through green and information technology", repeated Clinton in 2011.

In a speech given in November 2012, Clinton even referred to the TTP as "the gold standard in trade agreements". There is a video of this speech on YouTube, although the speech itself was removed from the website of the US Department of State. Despite these facts, Clinton tried to distance herself from the partnership during the elections. In one of the presidential debates, she claimed:

"The facts are I did say, I hoped it would be a good deal. But when it was negotiated, which I was not responsible for, I concluded it wasn't."

The truth is completely different. Not only she is on the record for praising TTP at least 45 times, but she also took a "leading part in drafting the Trans-Pacific Partnership", according to Bloomberg. However, when she faced political pressures along the campaign she had to come out and claim that she opposes the deal.

In order for you to realize why both NAFTA and TTP are bad things for the people of America, let's take a look at some of the reasons the experts offered:

- TTP would destroy America's sovereignty and independence – TTP means that international bureaucrats and judges would be in charge of making sure the treaty is followed and resolving all conflicts.
- TTP is planned in secrecy – the only parts of the agreement accessible to the public are the ones that leaked. Obama and his administration claimed the treaty is "completely transparent", although it was never published. On the other hand, pharmaceutical companies, Wall Street, Hollywood Studios and other corporate interests got the passwords to access the documents online. The fact that the process of planning the TTP was going on in secrecy baffled both Republicans and Democrats, which also criticized the decision to keep the treaty from the public and acting like there was nothing to hide.

- TTP is a corporatist scheme – globalist corporations are behind the TTP. They prefer to use the power of government than risk, innovation, and excellence to prosper. Free enterprise capitalists and regular people can't benefit from the agreement, it only serves big corporations. This claim goes in line with the previous one that only large corporations can access and study the TTP, while it's being kept a secret for the public.
- TTP is a regional transition in the push toward a world government

Towards the end of 2016, President of Turkey Recep Tayyip Erdogan claimed on multiple occasions that he has evidence that the United States and the coalition they lead have supported ISIS, as well as Kurdish militant groups PYD and YPG.

"They accused us of supporting Daesh (Islamic State). Now they give support to them and other terrorist groups. It's very clear and we have confirmed evidence".

Although Erdogan didn't actually publish any evidence, it was clear that the United States are reluctant to provide the support to Russia and Turkey that joined forces in attacking ISIS. It became clear why when Washington watchdog group Judicial Watch published evidence that supported the claims that the US-led coalition armed ISIS. Hillary Clinton played one of the main roles in the process and even invited to additionally arm the opposition Syrian army on more than one occasion.

Judicial Watch filed a lawsuit against the Department of Defense and secured the release of the reports that confirmed that Obama knew that weapons were shipped from the Port of Benghazi to rebel forces in Syria and that Clinton is behind it. WikiLeaks released an e-mail that Hillary Clinton, serving as a Secretary of State, sent to John Podesta on August 17, 2014:

"At the same time, we should return to plans to provide the FSA [Free Syria Army], with some group of moderate forces, with equipment that will allow them to deal with a weakened ISIL, and stepped up operations against the Syrian regime."

Andrew C. McCarthy, a senior policy fellow at the National Review Institute, tied Clinton's e-mail comment to the weapon shipment from Benghazi to Turkey for eventual transit to Syria in 2012. McCarthy further noted that the shipment of weapons had been arranged by Marc Turi, a professional arms dealer who had been indicted by federal prosecutors in Phoenix for supplying arms to Libyan "rebels" during the 2010-2011 war.

However, Obama's administration dropped the criminal case just one day before a court-ordered deadline to disclose information about its efforts to arm Muslim rebels.

"Turi's lawyers had explained his defense to the court: His arms shipments, destined for the Libyan rebels and channeled through Qatar and the United Arab Emirates, were part of a U.S.-authorized effort," McCarthy wrote. "Turi further asserts that the Obama administration was subsequently complicit in the shipment of weapons from Libya to 'rebels' in Syria, who are fighting the Assad regime."

Judge Andrew Napolitano, Fox News' senior judicial analyst, insisted that the Department of Justice had to drop the prosecution of Turi or his defense would expose Clinton's secret weapons running to the radical al-Qaida-affiliated rebels in Libya.

"Secretary Clinton decided she had to get rid of Gadhafi because she wanted to take credit when she ran for president for being the government official responsible for liberating Libya," Napolitano said.

Clinton knew she would never get a declaration of war from the Congress or authorization under the war powers resolution enacted over President Nixon's veto in 1973.

"So, Secretary Clinton persuaded Obama to use CIA intelligence assets who would be exempted from the war powers resolution even if they wore military fatigues in Libya."

Napolitano explained that to use intelligence assets under the war powers resolution, Clinton needed the cooperation and informal consent of the "Congress within the Congress," referring to the House Committee on Intelligence and the Senate Select Committee on Intelligence, which are both sworn to secrecy.

"The result is the president of the United States, the secretary of state and about two dozen people in the House and Senate, including the leadership of both parties in both houses, can authorize a clandestine war using CIA assets," he said.

"And this is exactly what President Obama and Secretary Clinton did."

After securing the authorization of the House and Senate intelligence committees, Clinton started a secret operating of shipping weapons to Libya.

I should also mention the irony of the whole process of the Turi's prosecution. He never actually shipped any weapons to Libya, but prosecuting him for planning to do so was what Clinton and Obama planned to the in case that the Secretary Clinton's clandestine arms dealings ever become public.

Chapter 3: George Soros

A Radical Non-Jewish Jew and Why He Wants to Hurt People

High-profile politicians are the ones that receive the most attention, but people tend to forget the "puppet masters" behind them. Those are billionaires with enough money to push their agenda. When it comes to Obama, Hillary and other politicians that spread fear and killed people around the world, they have one major source where the money comes from. It's a radical leftist billionaire called George Soros. He doesn't care about the well-being of people in America and across the globe. Soros has only two goals – to increase his wealth and his influence.

Soros made his fortune thanks to risky currency trades. That was not always fair game as he often made sure to secure the profit. He largely contributed to the Asian financial crisis in 1997, when several currencies across the continent collapsed. He managed to cause troubles in many countries of the world and only rare were smart like Russia, which banned Soros Foundation in time, describing it as a "threat to the constitutional order and national security".

As for the influence, Soros himself claimed on multiple occasions:

"I admit that I have always harbored an exaggerated view of my self-importance. To put it bluntly, I fancied myself as some kind of god. I carried strong messianic fantasies from my childhood, which I felt I needed to control or I could end up in the loony bin".

Despite being a Jew himself, Soros comes from an anti-Semitic family. He was a Nazi collaborator known for confiscating property from Jews as a teenager.

"My mother was shamed for being Jewish and she was quite anti-Semitic. Being a Jew was a handicap and a clear-cut stigma, which is why there was always the desire to escape it. I don't deny Jews their national existence, but I don't want to be a part of it", said Soros in an interview with the New Yorker.

Dennis Prager describes Soros as a non-Jewish Jew, an individual that was born a Jew but refuses to be identified that way (keep in mind that Judaism is not a religious identity, but a national/peoplehood one). Soros doesn't accept American roots either. Instead, he considers himself as a citizen of the world without any religious or national identity. As such, he uses political influence to undermine the religious and national roots of others.

People who reject their roots are often most violent towards their own national and religious groups. Ex-Catholics are the ones who harbor the greatest animosity toward the Catholic Church. The same way, those who reject their Jewish and American identities are far more likely to hurt their own group. A non-Jewish Jew might claim that he loves humanity, but in reality, he hurts humans.

The Media Research Center's report from 2011 confirmed Soros' ties to more than 30 news outlets in the mainstream media. We'll just take one example – at the time of the report, Soros funded Pro-Publica's Journalism Advisory board with Jill Abramson, former executive editor of The New York Times which is a now a columnist for The Guardian, and Kerry Smith, the senior vice president for editorial quality of ABC News.

Other media members on boards of similar Soros-funded advisory groups are:

- Ben Sherwood – ABC News president
- Michele Norris – host of "All Things Considered", public radio's longest-running national program
- Christiane Amanpour - CNN's chief international correspondent
- George Osterkamp – CBS News producer
- Len Downie – Vice President of the Washington Post

Soros also funds the Media Matters organization, which numerous media outlets, such as The New York Times and The Los Angeles Times, use for content. The task of this group is to hyperventilate over any conservative view that makes it into the mainstream media. The organization has recently declared an open war on Fox News, a weird mission for a tax-exempt educational foundation which should be barred from participating in the partisan political activity.

Why did Soros build up a conglomerate of political and media organizations?

He wants to influence public policy and the mainstream media. On more than one occasion, he used them to manipulate media coverage of election issues.

The whole process works like this: Brennan Center for Justice, an organization funded by Soros's companies, releases a claim that there is no voter fraud. That idea is then picked up and pushed into the public by the media that Soros also controls. The majority of the big media corporations publish news that corresponds to Soros' ambitions or point of views, thus achieving the goal of influencing the public. On the other hand, there is no room for news that may offer a different point of view.

George Soros was the biggest funder of the Hillary Clinton's campaign for the elections in 2016 that she lost to Donald Trump. Leaked emails proved intensive communication between John Podesta, Clinton's campaign manager and Soros' Open Society Foundations (OSF). The billionaire contributed $8 million to the political action committee (PAC) associated with Clinton. He also donated $2 million to American Bridge 21st Century, an organization that openly targeted Trump. Immigrant Voters Win received $3 million from Soros' OSF with the idea to mobilize Hispanic voters across key swing states.

There are reports that Soros went that far to stop Trump that he donated $488,375 to John Kasich, another Republican presidential candidate that tried to secure GOP nomination. The Color of Change is a race related organization also funded by the billionaire. Members of this organization collected signatures for a petition demanding major corporate sponsors to withdraw from the Republican National Convention. It worked as several of them completely retreated, while Coke contributed only $65,000, almost ten times less than in 2012. The Color of Change's mission is to defund law enforcement agencies that don't defend black lives. They received $500,000 for their effort during the campaign.

Why did Soros do this? As I mentioned before, he has the God complex and, as such, he always seeks to be the man in charge. The billionaire chooses politicians that are willing to be his puppets, something that Trump didn't accept.

It's not only the presidential elections that Soros meddles in. As part of his effort to overhaul the justice system of the United States, he donated to several law enforcement races throughout the country. The billionaire gave just under $10 million to defeat white Republican male DAs and replace them with minorities that favor a radical transformation of the system. He didn't take any chances, so he also funded Democratic primaries to make that the most radical Democrat won.

Soros spent a total of $2.3 million just to defeat the Arizona county Sheriff Joe Arpaio since he didn't like his tough approach to fighting illegal immigration. At the end of the race, Arpaio lost to Paul Penzone, an unknown Democrat challenger with a history of domestic violence involving his ex-wife.

Another way that Soros rigged the elections in 2016 are the lawsuits challenging election integrity laws in North Carolina, Ohio, and Wisconsin. He poured big money and managed to put the strict requirement of the North Carolina Law to have a "fresh photo-ID, shaved a week off of early voting, and cut same-day registration, preregistration and out of precinct voting. His grants also led to California and Oregon moving toward mandatory voter registration, where all people that are on a government database are automatically placed on the eligible voters' list.

Soros spends big money to fund organizations that hype up cries of racism. The most famous organization is certainly Black Lives Matter, a race related organization that claims the Republicans want to disenfranchise minorities. BLM is famous for celebrating the sniper attack in Dallas when five white police officers were killed in cold blood for no good reason. The idea behind these organizations is to radicalize minorities and rally them to vote and influence other registered voters to support far left candidates.

The billionaire's efforts didn't stop even after America had chosen Trump. On the contrary, he started organizing protests through his organizations. The famous "Women's March" in 2017 was everything but a non-partisan's protest, although they bragged with the independent organization. There was a total of 403 "partners' of the march and, according to the in-depth research of the New York Times' reporter Asra Q. Nomani, at least 56 of them receive their funding or have a close relationship with Soros. These organizations include MoveOn.org (which was strongly pro-Clinton during the campaign) and the National Action Network (the organization placed a man that has close contacts with Obama's administration as a co-chair of the march). Other known partners of the march are Amnesty International, American Civil Liberties Union, and Human rights watch, all funded by Soros. As a professional journalist, Nomani tried to ask them for a comment on the story, but they failed to answer to hew queries.

Conclusion

References

http://www.infowars.com/obama-retaliates-against-russians-over-purported-cyberattack-but-is-therea-double-standard/

https://www.intellihub.com/georgia-sec-of-state-trump-investigate-dhs-over-hack/

https://obamawhitehouse.archives.gov/the-press-office/2015/04/01/executive-order-blockingproperty-certain-persons-engaging-significant-m

http://www.infowars.com/woman-power-hillary-clinton-gave-order-to-murder-waco-babies/

http://www.economicpolicyjournal.com/2014/01/hillary-ordered-final-massacre-at-waco.html

http://www.history.com/this-day-in-history/federal-agents-raid-the-branch-davidian-compound-inwaco-texas

http://www.dailymail.co.uk/news/article-3753013/Missing-FBI-files-linking-Hillary-Clinton-suicideWhite-House-counsel-Vince-Foster-vanished-National-Archives.html

http://dailycaller.com/2017/01/07/young-obama-voter-says-race-relations-worse-after-8-years-ofamericas-first-black-president-video/

http://www.dailywire.com/news/12230/complete-timeline-race-relations-under-obama-harrykhachatrian#

http://www.infowars.com/us-led-coalition-admits-killing-at-least-188-civilians-in-syria-iraq/

http://www.infowars.com/foreign-lawmakers-slam-assassin-obama-over-drone-strikes/

http://www.infowars.com/murder-by-drone-obama-to-announce-civilian-death-toll-numbers-buttheres-a-catch/

https://www.yahoo.com/news/obama-lawyers-citizens-targeted-war-us-154313473.html?ref=gs

https://www.theguardian.com/us-news/2016/jul/01/obama-drones-strikes-civilian-deaths

https://www.theatlantic.com/politics/archive/2016/12/president-obamas-weak-defense-of-his-recordon-drone-strikes/511454/

https://www.thebureauinvestigates.com/2016/07/01/obama-drone-casualty-numbers-fractionrecorded-bureau/

http://www.dennisprager.com/george-soros-and-the-problem-of-the-radical-non-jewish-jew/

http://humanevents.com/2011/04/02/top-10-reasons-george-soros-is-dangerous/

http://www.mrc.org/special-reports/george-soros-media-mogul

http://www.dailywire.com/news/8427/9-things-you-need-know-about-george-soros-aaron-bandler#

http://pointofview.net/articles/soros-manipulated-election/

http://www.infowars.com/sick-black-lives-matter-supporters-celebrate-murder-of-dallas-cops/

http://nytlive.nytimes.com/womenintheworld/2017/01/20/billionaire-george-soros-has-ties-to-more-than-50-partners-of-the-womens-march-on-washington/

http://dailycaller.com/2016/10/07/leaked-emails-show-clinton-campaign-coordinating-with-soros-organization/

https://www.thenewamerican.com/usnews/constitution/item/21010-10-reasons-why-you-should-oppose-obamatrade

https://www.bloomberg.com/news/articles/2013-01-10/how-hillary-clinton-created-a-u-s-business-promotion-machine

http://www.snopes.com/hillary-clinton-called-trans-pacific-partnership-the-gold-standard/

http://www.breitbart.com/2016-presidential-race/2016/09/26/fact-check-clinton-lies-support-tpp/

http://www.zerohedge.com/news/2016-12-24/obama-signs-countering-disinformation-and-propaganda-act-law

http://www.snopes.com/obama-signs-christmas-bill-making-alternative-media-illegal/

http://www.infowars.com/breaking-obama-bans-free-speech-in-the-dead-of-night/

http://www.wnd.com/2017/01/leaked-audio-obama-wanted-isis-to-grow/

https://www.nytimes.com/interactive/2016/09/30/world/middleeast/john-kerry-syria-audio.html?_r=0

https://theconservativetreehouse.com/2017/01/01/absolutely-stunning-leaked-audio-of-secretary-kerry-reveals-president-obama-intentionally-allowed-rise-of-isis/comment-page-4/#comments

http://www.wnd.com/2015/05/declassified-docs-hillary-aided-rise-of-isis/

http://www.wnd.com/2016/12/evidence-backs-erdogans-claim-that-hillary-armed-isis/

http://www.judicialwatch.org/press-room/press-releases/judicial-watch-defense-state-department-documents-reveal-obama-administration-knew-that-al-qaeda-terrorists-had-planned-benghazi-attack-10-days-in-advance/